About the Author

The author was born in a hillside village in Sicily and immigrated to Canada in the late fifties with her family. She was one of eight children. The death of her two young sisters left her with a deep sadness and continues to influence her life. She is a graduate of theatre and formed a number of theatre companies after she graduated. She has trained actors in Canada, India and New York City for over twenty years as well as successfully producing video. This is her first work to be published.

LOVE BEADS

Asee N Silla

LOVE BEADS

Vanguard Press

VANGUARD PAPERBACK

© Copyright 2023
Asee N Silla

The right of Asee N Silla to be identified as author of this work has been asserted by her in accordance with the Copyright, Designs and Patents Act 1988.

All Rights Reserved

No reproduction, copy or transmission of this publication may be made without written permission.
No paragraph of this publication may be reproduced, copied or transmitted save with the written permission of the publisher, or in accordance with the provisions of the Copyright Act 1956 (as amended).

Any person who commits any unauthorised act in relation to this publication may be liable to criminal prosecution and civil claims for damages.

A CIP catalogue record for this title is available from the British Library.

ISBN 978 1 80016 624 0

*Vanguard Press is an imprint of
Pegasus Elliot Mackenzie Publishers Ltd.*
www.pegasuspublishers.com

First Published in 2023

**Vanguard Press
Sheraton House Castle Park
Cambridge England**

Printed & Bound in Great Britain

SECTION 1 – THE UNVEILING

BEAD I

She didn't mean to fall in love with him
But she did
It happened innocuously innocently

She was married
A 43-year-old woman
A 43-year-old woman with children and a husband
She was married

She loved her husband
Or so she thought
She wasn't sure
And so she stayed

She stayed
She stayed in the marriage
She stayed with her husband
She stayed with her family

Was it obligation
Was it religion
Was it her parents

It must have been her parents
They would be disappointed
If she left they would be disappointed

She made the best of it
The perfect family
The perfect home
The perfect children

Everyone saw the happiness
Everyone saw the joy
Everyone saw that things were just right
She made everything just right

But she wasn't happy
She wasn't happy with herself
She wasn't happy with him

Who was he
Who was her husband
Who was she
Who was this wife
He didn't know
She didn't know

Was it the disappointments
Was it the broken promises
Was it the misunderstandings

She just didn't know

She knew
Shortly into the marriage
She knew
Shortly into the marriage
Something was not right
Shortly into the marriage
Something was not certain
Shortly into the marriage
Something was too rushed
She knew
In her dreams she knew
And she stayed

She gave her promise
She gave her word
Her promise was eternal
Her word was gold

He loved her
So he said
He said he loved her
So she stayed

She stayed in hope
She stayed in hope of change
She stayed so things would get better
She stayed so he would get better

She stayed so she would get better

And then he came
She didn't mean to fall in love with him
But she did

He came from India
He came with his wife from India
He came with his wife to live in Canada
He came to experience life in Canada

His wife was her friend
His wife was a friend from school
His wife met him in India
His wife flirted with him in India
His wife married him in India

His wife brought him to Canada
His wife wanted him to know Canada
His wife wanted him to experience Canada

His wife was her friend
His wife introduced them
His wife sparked the match

His wife didn't know what she had done
His wife didn't see what she had done
His wife didn't hear what she had done

He liked her
He liked his wife's friend
He seemed to know his wife's friend
He seemed to understand his wife's friend
He seemed to care for his wife's friend
He seemed to care for the married 43-year-old
woman

The man from India stayed for a year
The man from India tried for a year
The man from India was a good husband for a year

But the man from India didn't like the cold
The man from India didn't like the snow
The man didn't like being dark in Canada

After a year he left
After a year he went back to India
After a year he went back to his people
After a year he went back to his land
After a year he went back to the heat

His wife followed him
His wife followed him back to India
His wife followed him back to the heat

His wife became pregnant
His wife wanted the child in Canada
His wife wanted their child born in Canada

They returned to Canada
Her friend and her husband returned to Canada
They returned to have a child in Canada
They returned to have the child born in Canada

The child was born
The child was born in Canada
The child would be a citizen of Canada
The child would be free to stay in Canada

She saw the child in Canada
She saw her friend in Canada
She saw her friend leave
She saw her friend leave with her child
She saw her friend bring her child to India

She stayed in Canada
The 43-year-old woman stayed in Canada
She stayed in her marriage in Canada
She stayed with her family in Canada

She thought of him
She thought of the man from India
She thought of her friend's husband

She would not see him
She would never see him again
She would never be with him again

She would never see the man from India again

It took three years
It took three years for his wife to leave him
It took three years for things to fall apart
It took three years for his wife to leave India

His wife left India
His wife returned to Canada
His wife brought their child to Canada

He stayed in India
He stayed in India where he longed for his family
He stayed in India longing for his child in Canada
He stayed in India wanting his child in India

Her friend arrived
Her friend arrived in Canada
Her friend came to start a new life in Canada

She met her friend
She met her friend in Canada
She met her friend's child in Canada

She listened to her friend's disappointment
She listened to her friend's disillusionment
She listened to her friend's disappointment with her
husband in India

She liked her friend's child
She played with her friend's child
She laughed with her friend's child
She spent time looking after her friend's child

Her friend's child loved her
Her friend's child liked being with her
Her friend's child was relaxed with her

She was happy to be with her friend's child
She was happy to share her children with her friend's child
She was happy she became a friend to her friend's child

The child did not see her father
The child in Canada did not see her father
The child in Canada did not see her father in India

At last he came to visit
He came to visit his child
He came to visit his child in Canada

He came to play with his child
He came to know his child
He came to love his child

For a few days
He would be with his child

For a few days
The child would be with him
For a few days he would be a father

A few days does not a father make
A few days does not a daughter make
A few days does not the love of a daughter make

The child did not know him
The child was afraid to be with him
The child was afraid to be alone with her father

The child wanted her
The child wanted her to be with them
The child wanted her to be with her and her father

She loved the child
She obeyed the child
She came to please the child
She came to be with the child and her father

And so it started
She visited the child
He visited his child
She was with the child and her father
She got to know the father
She came to love the father
She came to love the child and her father

BEAD II

They went for walks
Together they went for walks
She, the child and the child's father went for walks

They walked
They talked
She, the child and the child's father walked and talked

When the child went off to play
They talked
She and the child's father talked
She and the child's father shared
She and the child's father shared their disappointments
She and the child's father shared the disappointments in their marriage

He was unhappy
She was unhappy
She and the child's father were unhappy
She and the child's father were unhappy in their marriage

She listened
She heard

He listened
He heard

They listened and heard
They listened and heard each other's loneliness
She and the child's father listened
They heard each other's loneliness

His wife was her friend
Her friend was his child's mother
The child's mother was still his wife
He was devoted to his wife
In his loneliness
He was devoted to his wife

She told him patience
She told him to be patient with his wife
She advised him to listen to his wife
She advised him to love his wife

BEAD III

The first visit passed quickly
He left his child
The man from India left his child
He left his child and his wife
He left her
He left to go back to India

She stayed
She stayed with her sons
She stayed with her husband
She stayed in Canada

She was not happy
He was not happy
She did not see him
He did not see her

She saw his child
He did not see his child

BEAD IV

He missed his child
He longed for his child
He missed his wife
He was devoted to his wife

He longed for his family
In India he longed for his family
He longed for his family in Canada

Her friend was angry
She was angry with her husband
She was angry with her husband in India

She rejected him
She rejected her husband in India
She belittled her husband in India
She betrayed her husband in India

He was angry
He was angry with his wife
He was angry with his wife in Canada
He was angry with his wife in Canada who betrayed
him

He longed for his child
He longed for the child he left in Canada
He longed for the family he left in Canada

He was proud
He was a proud man
He was a proud Hindu man
He was a proud Hindu man in India

For his child he swallowed his pride
For his child he swallowed his hurt
For his child he returned to Canada

He saw his child
He saw his child in Canada
He was happy to be with his child in Canada

His child saw him
His child did not know him
His child was afraid of him
His child would not be alone with him in Canada

His child wanted her
His child wanted her to be with them
His child wanted her to be with her and her father

She came for the child
She came so the child would not be alone

She came so the child would not be alone with her
father

She was happy to see him
She was happy to be with his child
She was happy to be with him and his child
She was happy he came to Canada

He needed a place
He needed a place to stay
He needed a place to stay to be near his child

His wife had a place
His wife had a place with her child
His wife would not let him stay with her and his
child

He stayed with her
He stayed with her in her home
He stayed in her home in the basement
He stayed with her in the apartment in her home

He ate with her
He ate with her and her husband
He ate with her and her husband and sons

He liked her family
He liked her husband
He liked her sons

He stayed with her and her family

She was happy
She was happy he stayed with her
She was happy he stayed with her and her family

They made plans
They made plans to travel
They made plans to travel for the child
They made plans to travel together with his child

And so it started
The traveling started
For the child the traveling started
For the child they traveled together

They traveled to Toronto
They traveled to Niagara
They traveled to Stratford

They saw plays
They saw movies
They saw dolphins

She was happy to be with his child
He was happy to be with his child
The child was happy to be with her father
The child was happy to be with her

She was happy to be with him
He was happy to be with her
He was happy to be with her and his child

The second visit was short
He went back to India
He went back to his people
He went back to his heat

She stayed in Canada
His child stayed in Canada
His wife stayed in Canada

And so it continued
Year after year he came
Year after year he visited his child
Year after year he traveled with his child
Year after year she traveled with them
Year after year they traveled together

She was happy with them
She was happy to travel with them
She was happy to travel with him and his child
His child loved to travel
His child loved to travel with her
His child loved to travel with her and her father
His child loved that they were together
His child wanted her to be with her father

She still had her husband
He still had his wife
She befriended him
He befriended her
They befriended each other

He lived in India
She lived in Canada

BEAD V

She wanted to be happy
She wanted her husband to be happy
She wanted her marriage to be happy
She wanted her family to be happy

She didn't know
She didn't know what to do
She didn't know how to be
She didn't know what happiness felt like
She didn't know

She felt alone
She felt alone with her husband
She felt unheard by her husband
She felt abandoned by her husband
Though he was always present
She felt abandoned

She tried
She tried to be happy
She tried to make her husband happy
She did everything to make her husband happy

She went to her doctor
She talked to her doctor
She told her doctor of her unhappiness
She told her doctor of her husband
She told her doctor she did everything to make her husband happy

The doctor surprised her
The doctor's words were news to her
The doctor's words broke through to her

Your job is not to make your husband happy
Your job is to find your own happiness
Your job is to share your happiness
Your job is to share your happiness with your husband

This is what the doctor told her
This is what the doctor counseled her
This is how the doctor consoled her

She told her husband
She told her husband the doctor's words
She told her husband the doctor's counsel

Her husband was not pleased
Her husband was not pleased with the doctor
Her husband was not pleased with the doctor's counsel

Her husband was unhappy
Her husband wanted her to make him happy
Her husband wanted the marriage to make him
happy

Her husband had been unhappy for a long time
Her husband had been lost for a long time
Her husband had been rebelling for a long time

She didn't know how to make her husband happy
She didn't know how to make herself happy
She didn't know how to make the marriage happy

BEAD VI

A year passed
After a year he came back
In the summer he came back
He came back from India
He came back for his child

He stayed with her
He stayed with her in her house
He stayed with her in her empty house

Her husband was away
Her sons were away
She was alone in the house
She was alone with him in her house

She was happy to be with him

His child came
His child came to visit in her house
His child came to visit in her empty house

They made meals together
They walked together
They talked together

At night the child left
At night the child went back to her mother
At night they were left alone
At night they were left alone in her empty house

The fire was lit
The fire was burning quietly
The fire broke the silence
The fire broke the silence of the empty house

They watched the fire
They sat and watched the fire burn
Sipping cognac they sat and watched the fire burn

Sipping cognac they talked
Sipping cognac they laughed
Sipping cognac they shared their lives

This was new to her
This was a surprise to her
This was strange to her
In front of the fire he listened
In front of the fire he heard
In front of the fire he understood
In front of the fire he understood her

This never happened
This never happened with her husband
This never happened in her marriage
This never happened in her life

This was a first
This was the first time she was with a man
This was the first time she was alone with a man in her home
This was the first time she was alone with a man
She was alone in her home with a man who was not her husband
This was the first time she was with a man and not fighting
This was the first time she was alone with a man in front of the fire

And then it happened
She looked at him
She listened to him
She saw him
She saw him like she had never seen anyone before

The veil lifted
The veil she never knew she had lifted
The veil in front of her eyes lifted
The veil lifted and for the first time she saw

She saw him
She saw the man in front of her
She saw her friend's husband as a man
She saw the man she wanted for the first time

Something changed
She wanted him
She wanted him like she had never wanted someone before

Her pores tingled
The hairs on her arms stood on ends
She wanted to move close to him
She wanted him to move close to her

She said nothing
She did nothing
He said nothing
He did nothing

The innocence remained
It was time to sleep
They said their goodbyes
He went to the basement
She went to her room

The veil had lifted
In her room she couldn't breathe
In her room she wanted him

In her room she needed him
In her room she sighed for him

In her room he became her air
In her room he became her breath
In her room he became her reason to live

She longed for him
She longed for the impossible
She longed for someone who was not hers

BEAD VII

She lay in bed
In her room she lay in bed
In her bed she felt a sensation
In her bed she felt a longing
In her room she felt a sensation

What was this longing
What was this sensation
Why didn't she have it with her husband
Why didn't she have it in her marriage

Why now
Why not before
She knew why
She knew the reason
She knew she was heard
She knew she was understood

These sensations were new
These sensations were foreign
These sensations tingled
These sensations gave her a new found life

She thought of him
She thought of the man from India
She couldn't stop thinking about the man from
India

She went to him
She went to the basement
She went to his room in the basement

She knocked on his door
Ever so gently she knocked on his door
She stood by his door
She thought by his door
She thought of him by his door
By his door she thought of him awake
By his door she thought of him asleep

She knocked again
She listened again
She heard him again

She spoke to him
Outside his bedroom she spoke to him
She told him
She told him about her longing
She told him about the unveiling
She told him about the sensations

He invited her into his room
She hesitated
She was unsure
She went in
She lay beside him

He massaged her feet
She massaged his
He told her he couldn't
He told her he respected her husband
He left her longing
He left her unsatisfied

She returned to her room
She returned to her room unsatisfied
Unsatisfied she returned to her room

He went back to India
He went back to his world

She stayed in Canada
She stayed with her family

She thought about him
She wrote to him

He thought about her
He wrote to her

He was concerned for her welfare
He cared for their friendship

She was concerned for him
She cared for their friendship

SECTION II – THE SEPARATION

BEAD VIII

Her husband returned
Her husband returned from his trip
Her husband returned from his bicycling trip

She met her husband
She met her husband at the station
She met her husband at the train station

He reached out
He reached out to hug her
He reached out to kiss her

She froze
She repelled
She spurned his advances

She could not touch him
She could not be with him
She could not stand being with him

He took her hand
Her husband took her hand

She pushed it away
She pushed his hand away
She pushed him away

They left the station
They left the train station
They left the station in silence
The left the station as strangers

In silence they went home.
In silence they ate their meal

BEAD IX

She found a mediator
She found a mediator for them
She found a mediator to listen to them
She found a mediator who could help them

She told her husband
She told her husband she was not happy
After twenty years of marriage she was not happy

She had called the mediator
She asked the mediator for help
She asked the mediator to help them with their marriage

The mediator came
The mediator met them
The mediator spoke to her
The mediator spoke to him

The mediator heard
The mediator heard the disappointment
The mediator heard the pain
The mediator told them to separate

Her husband was silent
Her husband didn't want to see
Her husband didn't want to listen
Her husband didn't want to hear

The mediator left
She was in tears
She knew the truth
She knew she didn't love her husband

She was sad
She was tired
She was sorry

Her husband was sad
Her husband was tired
Her husband was sorry

Her husband didn't know
Her husband didn't hear
Her husband didn't understand

Her husband was silent
Her husband was in shock
Her husband got up
Her husband got up and left

Her husband agreed
Her husband agreed that they should separate
They agreed to separate
They did separate

BEAD X

The children didn't know
The children needed to know
Children needed to be told
Together
She and her husband told the children

They told
Together they told the children
Together they cried with the children

Her husband left
In two weeks her husband left

She went back to work
Her children went back to school

At school nobody knew
At school nobody said anything
At school the children wanted normalcy
At school the children wanted the perfect family

Her children were silent
Her children were numbed
Her nuclear family was no more
Her nuclear family had exploded

Doors closed
Silence remained
Nothing was said

SECTION III – THE LOVER

BEAD XI

The apartment was empty
The apartment in the basement was empty
He had left the apartment in the basement empty

He had gone back to India
He had gone back to his people
He had gone back to his heat

The apartment was empty
The apartment needed a tenant

The man from India had a friend
His friend needed an apartment
His friend saw the apartment
His friend took the apartment in the basement

His friend became her tenant
His friend made her laugh
His friend liked her
His friend teased her
His friend wanted her

Time passed
She was alone
Her husband had left
He had gone back to India
She was alone with her children

His friend was there
His friend stayed in the basement
His friend stayed in her apartment in the basement

She liked fires
She liked laughing
She liked talking
She liked joking

His friend talked with her
In front of the fireplace they talked
In front of the fireplace they laughed
In front of the fireplace they joked

His friend attended to her
His friend cooked for her
His friend shopped with her
His friend cared for her

She liked the attention
She liked the caring
She liked how he made her feel
She liked being together with him

She like being together with his friend

In her marriage she wasn't attended
In her marriage she wasn't cared for
In her marriage they were together in silence
In her marriage she felt alone

She liked his friend's attentions
She needed his friend's attentions
She craved his friend's attentions
His friend's attentions made her feel special

She was happy
His friend was happy
His friend became her friend
His friend made her happy

The friendship continued
The friendship was good
The friendship created happiness
His friend knew his place
She knew his place
The friendship was something they both needed

He wanted more
His friend wanted more
The friend of the man from India wanted more
She wanted less
She wanted less from this friend

She still thought of him
She still thought of the man from India

BEAD XII

Soon it would be Christmas
Soon there would be snow
Soon there would be holidays
Soon there would be visits

She made the beds
She cleaned the house
She cooked the meals
She sent the invites

She was happy
He was coming
The man from India was coming
And she was happy

He was coming to visit his child
He was coming to visit her
He was coming for Christmas
He was coming to be with his child at Christmas

He didn't know
He didn't know about her
He didn't know about her husband

He didn't know that she slept alone

She wanted to surprise him
She wanted to be free
She wanted to be free with him
She wanted him to be free with her

He would stay with her
He would stay with her children
He would see his friend
He would see his friend in the basement
He would see his friend in the apartment in the
basement

BEAD XIII

She waited for him
Anxiously she waited for him
Happily she prepared her home for him
Lovingly she bought gifts for him
Lovingly she bought gifts for him and his child
He finally came
He arrived at the airport
He went through customs at the airport
He waited for his baggage at the airport

She went to the airport
She went to pick him up at the airport
She waited for him at the airport
She waited for him to pick up his bags at the airport

He came through
He came through the doors at the airport
With his luggage and hat he came through the doors
at the airport

She saw him
She smiled at him
He saw her

He smiled at her
He came to her
He hugged her
She hugged him
They smiled
Together they smiled

She told him of the separation
She told him of the mediator
She told him of her children

He was sad for her
He was sad for her marriage
He was sad for her children

He was not happy with his wife
He was less happy with separation
He was a devoted man
He was an unhappy devoted man to his wife

At her home they prepared the meal
At her home they put up the tree
At her home they set the table
At her home her family was coming

On Christmas Day her parents came
On Christmas Day her siblings came
On Christmas Day her children came
They came to eat the meal

They came to be together
On Christmas Day they came to be together

She invited her husband
She invited the father of her children
She invited him to share this Christmas meal
Though they were separated she invited him to the meal

She invited him to the meal
She invited her friend from India to the meal
She invited her friend from India and his friend to the Christmas meal

They helped with the Christmas meal
The man from India helped with the meal
His friend helped with the meal
Her husband helped with the meal

He set the table
The man from India set the table
The man from India brought a beautiful cloth for the table

His friend made the rice
The man from India's friend made the rice
His friend showed her what he was doing
His friend showed her to use plenty of water
His friend showed her how to cook the rice

Her husband cut the bread
Her husband cut the bread thinly
In thin slices he cut the bread
In thin slices he put the bread in the basket
In thin slices her husband put the bread in the
basket and served it

She was happy
She was happy with all of them
She was happy with the man from India
She was happy with his friend
She was happy with her husband

Each took turns making her happy
Each took turns setting the table
Each took turns serving the food
Each took turns cleaning the dishes

She was happy
For once, she felt accepted
For once, she felt respected
For once, she felt loved

They laughed a lot
They joked a lot
They teased her a lot
Her husband, the man from India and his friend
They made her happy

It was a good time
It was a good memory
It was captured in smiles
It was a captured in photos

They sat by the fireplace
They drank cognac by the fireplace
They shared stories by the fireplace
They were together by the fireplace

Her family didn't know
Her family didn't know about her
Her family didn't know about her husband
Her family didn't know about the separation
She didn't want her family to know

And so the night passed
Her husband left
Her husband went back to his apartment
His friend left
He went back to the basement
He left
The man from India left
He went to his room
He went to the room next to hers

BEAD XIV

Christmas ended
He went back
The man from India went back
He went back to his people
He went back to his heat

She stayed
She stayed in Canada
She stayed with her children
She stayed with his friend

She missed him
She missed the man from India
She missed him more than she could imagine

She wanted him
She wanted the man from India
She wanted to be with the man from India
She wanted to love the man from India
No one knew
Or so she thought

His friend knew
His friend in the basement knew
He knew of her love
He knew of her desire
And he waited
He waited for his time
His friend in the basement waited for his time

He was happy there
In the basement he was happy
In the basement he waited
In the basement he waited to make her happy

He teased her
He teased her about her love
He teased her about her longing
He teased her about her desire
And he laughed

He laughed at her
He laughed at her love
He laughed at her longing
He laughed at her desire

She denied her truth
She denied her love
She denied her longing
She denied her desire

She lied
She lied to keep her secret
She lied to keep face
She lied to keep her sanity
She didn't want anyone to know
She didn't want her children to know
She didn't want her friends to know
She didn't want his friend to know

But his friend knew
His friend saw
His friend heard her voice
In the basement he knew, his friend knew
And so she relented
She told his friend about her love
She told his friend about her desire
She told his friend about her longing

His friend mocked her
He knew the man from India
He knew of his pride
He knew the pride in the man from India

He told her he was a peacock
He told her the man from India was a peacock
He told her he was vain
The man from India was vain
He told her she could never win his heart
He told her she could never win the heart

She could never win the heart of the man from
India

She didn't believe him
She didn't want to believe him
She told him that her heart was true
She told him that her heart didn't lie
She told him that her love didn't lie

He laughed at her
His friend laughed at her
His friend in the basement apartment laughed at her
He knew her secret
He knew her wants
He wanted her
In time he would have her

He waited
His friend in the basement waited for her
He knew she would break
He knew in time she would be his
He knew how to play her
Like an instrument to his touch
He knew how to play her
He just had to wait
And wait he did

BEAD XV

It happened
One night it happened
She went to a party
He went with her to a party
His friend from the basement went with her to a
party

She danced at the party
She drank at the party
She was happy at the party
He danced with her at the party
He drank with her at the party
He was happy to be with her at the party

She was letting go
To the music she was letting go
All her sadness slipped away
All her tears dried up
The music moved her
The music moved her hips
The music moved her arms
The music moved her lips
Inside her body the music seeped

Something unleashed her
She was lost inside her body
She was lost inside her world
She was lost inside her music
She was lost inside the wine
The music and the wine unleashed her

He saw this
His friend from the basement saw this
He was waiting for this
He was waiting to take her home
He was waiting to unleash her some more

He brought her home
His friend from the basement brought her home

He gave her more wine
He drank more wine
Together they drank more wine
Together they intertwined their glasses
Together they intertwined their arms
Together they intertwined their kisses
Together they drank more wine

This was the moment
This was the moment he was waiting for
This was the moment his friend from the basement wanted

She didn't resist
When he took her in his arms
She didn't resist
When he carried her
She didn't resist
When he laid her on the bed
She didn't resist

BEAD XVI

On her bed he loved her
Gently softly he loved her
With delicate fingers he stroked her
With delicate breaths he aroused her

This was new for her
This was sweet for her
This took time for her
This took finesse for her
He touched her with finesse
He aroused her with finesse

For her this was not sex
For her this was not work
For her this was music
She was his instrument and he was playing her song

In her marriage everything took effort
In her marriage lips didn't touch
In her marriage bodies weren't aroused
In her marriage she was tired

He was patient with her
He was patient with her body
He was patient with his hand

He glided his hand along her body
Lightly gently he glided his hand
With his hand he soothed her body

He used his fingers
With his fingers he played her
With his fingers he played her notes
With his fingers he played notes she never knew she had

The notes were soft
The notes were gentle
The notes played melodies
The notes played melodies she'd long forgotten
Melodies lost in caves of the divine

And so it started
His friend from the basement left the basement apartment
His friend moved upstairs
His friend slept with her
Though he had his own room
His friend slept with her

He played her
She played him
In the caves of the divine they played
Bringing up forgotten melodies

SECTION IV – THE UNRAVELLING

BEAD XVII

She was happy
For a while she forgot him
For a while she forgot the man from India
For a while she loved him
For a while she loved the man from the basement
Who was no longer in the basement

She was happy with her man
She was happy with her man from the basement
She was happy with him
He became her lover
He knew
Her lover knew
Her lover knew that she still thought of him
Her lover knew that she still wanted him
Her lover knew that she still longed for the man
from India

Her lover accepted this
Her lover didn't quarrel with this
Her lover wasn't jealous of this
Her lover wanted her
And for a while
Her lover had her

For a while he was good to her
For a while he treated her
For a while he brought her places
For a while they went on trips
For a while she was happy

He lived with her now
He stayed with her in her room
Though his room was beside hers
He stayed with her in her room

Her children didn't like him
Her children didn't like her lover
Her children didn't trust him
Her children warned her
Her children warned her about her lover

She didn't listen
She was too happy to listen
She was too involved to listen
She was too absorbed in herself to listen
She was too involved with her lover to listen to her children

But then she started to notice
She started to notice little things
She started to notice little things she thought endearing
Little things she thought funny

Little things she thought careless

They would be out
They would be out for dinner
They would be out to enjoy a nice meal

He was supposed to pay
He was supposed to pay the bill
He was supposed to pay for their time together

But he forgot his wallet
Look as he did he couldn't find his wallet
But then he remembered
He remembered it at home
He remembered he left it in his room

He used her car
He was always using her car
They would drive to the country
They would drive to the country with her car

They would run out of gas
They would run out of gas in her car
They would run out of gas in her car that he was
using

He would use her cell phone
He would always use her cell phone
He would always use her cell phone as his

Though she would pay the bill

And so it continued
She was always paying
She was always paying for these little things
She was always paying for things he never had money for

The more she paid
The less he cared
The more she carried him
The more he wanted from her

This made her feel uneasy
This made her feel used
This made her feel little
This made her feel like a fool

And then he made demands
He made demands on her time
He made demands on her attention
He made demands on her activities

He wanted her to do everything for him
He wanted her to write for him
He wanted her to buy for him
He wanted her to do projects for him

BEAD XVIII

She didn't want to do projects for him
She didn't want to support his goals
She didn't trust his treatment of her

    She had her own work
    She had her own goals
    She had her own dreams

He didn't want her work
He didn't want her goals
He didn't want her dreams

He wanted her for him
He wanted her to serve him
He wanted her to make him king

They started to argue
They started to fight
They started to ignore each other

She felt used by him
She felt hurt by him
She felt frustrated with him

She didn't know what to do
She didn't know what to say
She didn't know how to be with him

She stopped playing with him
He stopped playing with her
They stopped playing together

She asked him to leave
She asked him to leave her room
She asked him to leave her house
She asked him to leave her home

He said he would go
He said he would leave
He said he would leave her home
He said many things but he still stayed
The more he said he would leave
The more he stayed
The more he stayed
The more she was afraid

She wrote him letters
She wrote him letters to leave
She wrote him letters to go
She wrote him many letters
But still he stayed

She went to her lawyer
She went to her lawyer to write him letters
She went to her lawyer to write him letters to leave

Still he did not leave
Still he did not go
Still he made her home his

Days turned into weeks
Weeks turned into months
And still he did not go

She went on holidays
She went on holidays with friends
She went on holidays to get away
She went on holidays to get away from him

He stayed
He stayed in her home
He stayed in her home while she was away

Her holidays wouldn't last
Her holidays would end
Her holidays would end soon
Her ending holidays would force her back
Her ending holidays would force her back to him

She was afraid
She was afraid of him

She was afraid that he would take
She was afraid that he would take everything she had

Her work would start soon
Soon she'd be enmeshed in courses
Soon she'd be staying late
Soon she'd marking for hours

She was afraid to work
She was afraid to return to her job
She was afraid to return to her job with him in the house

With her job she would have no time
With her job she would get distracted
With her job she couldn't get him to leave
With her job he would stay in the house

She was in a panic
She was in a state of anxiety
She had done everything she could to get him to leave

He would not leave
He would not leave her
He would not leave her house

If he stayed he would own her
If he stayed he would control her
If he stayed he would claim her and her house

BEAD XIX

She made a decision
She made a decision about him
She made a decision that would make him leave
With her friends she would make him leave

She waited
She waited till he left
She waited till he left for work
She waited till he left the house

She packed his things
Her and her friends packed his things
Her and her friends packed all his things from everywhere

They packed his clothes
They packed his books
They packed his spices
They packed his food
They packed his pots

They put them in boxes
Her and her friends put all his things in boxes

Her and her friends put all the boxes outside
Outside her home they put all his boxes

She changed the locks
She changed the locks to all the doors
She changed the locks to all the doors in her house

She was anxious
She was fearful
She didn't want to lose her home
She didn't want to
But she changed the locks

She knew
She knew what he would do
She knew if she didn't do this
She knew he would stay with her
She knew he would stay with her in her home
She knew he would never leave her

She knew
So she packed his clothes
She knew so she packed the boxes
She knew so she changed the locks

She knew
If he stayed with her
She would not be free

She knew
If he stayed with her
Her spirit would die
She knew
If he stayed with her
She would lose everything

So she changed the locks
She left her house

BEAD XX

He returned home
He came back to her house
He saw his things
Outside the house he saw his things

He tried his keys
He turned his keys
His keys would not go in the lock
His keys would not open the door

He knocked
He knocked on the door
He knocked on the door of the house
He knocked on the door of an empty house

He waited
He waited for her to come
He waited for her to open the door

He listened
He listened for her to come
He listened for her to come to open the door

She did not come
Though he waited and listened
She did not come

He looked through the windows
He looked through the windows of the house
He looked through the windows of the empty house
He did not see her

He panicked
Outside the house he panicked
Outside the house he did not know what to do

He walked
He left the house and walked
Up and down he walked in front of the empty house

He decided
He decided to take his things
He decided to put his things in the car
He decided to put his things in the car and leave

BEAD XXI

She came back
The next day she came back
She came back to her house
She came back to her home

She saw
She saw his things were gone
She saw his things were not there

She was relieved
She was relieved that he was gone
She was relieved that he was no longer in the house
She was relieve that he was no longer in her home

He came back
Later that day he came back
He came back to speak to her
He came back to reason with her

He tried to reach her
He tried to comfort her
He wanted to comfort her
He wanted to embrace her

She was cold
She would not speak with him
She would not listen to him
She would not listen to her former lover
She would not listen to her former friend
She would not listen to her former friend and lover

He left her
Her former lover left her
No smiles would touch her
No words would move her
No kisses would comfort her
He finally left her

SECTION V – DIVIDED LOYALTIES

BEAD XXII

He came back
The man from India came back
The man from India came back for Christmas
He came back to be with his child at Christmas

He didn't like the cold
He didn't like the ice
He didn't like the snow
But he came back
He came to be with his child at Christmas

He did not stay with her
The man from India did not stay in her house
He did not stay in her home
He did not stay with her family

He knew what happened
He knew what happened to his friend
He knew what his friend had told him
He knew what his friend had said about her

He was not happy with her
The man from India was not happy with her
He did not like what she had done
He did not like what she could do
He did not like what she had done to his friend

She explained
She explained her actions
She justified her actions
She justified her actions to the man from India

He did not listen
He would not listen
The man from India would not listen

He was afraid of her
He was afraid of her and loyal to his friend
He was loyal to his friend, her former lover

He stayed at an inn
This Christmas he stayed at an inn
He would not stay with her
Because of his loyalty
He would not stay with her

This upset her
This upset her very much
She wanted to be close to him
She wanted to be close to the man from India

BEAD XXIII

He visited his friend
The man from India visited his friend
He left his child to visit his friend

He was loyal
The man from India was loyal
The man from India was loyal to his friend

He would not betray his friend
The man from India would not betray his friend

He would not love her
He couldn't love her
He didn't love her
To love her would betray his friend
He would not betray his friend

She went to see him
She went to see the man from India
She went to see the man from India at the inn

She brought his child
She brought his child to the inn
She brought the child to the man from India

They laughed together
They were happy together
They made meals together
They ate together

The child liked her
The child told her father
The child told her father to marry her
The child said they were good together

The man from India listened to his child
The man from India disagreed with his child
The man from India would not marry her

He didn't want to marry
He wouldn't marry her just to please his child
He wouldn't marry anyone just to please his child

He was disappointed with her
He didn't like what she had done to his friend
He would be loyal to his friend
He would not love her

She heard him
She heard him speak to his child
She heard him speak of loyalty
She heard and trembled

She heard and trembled as her heart broke

She loved his child
She loved him
But he was loyal to his friend
He was loyal to her ex-lover

How could she love him
How could she love him if he didn't love her
How could her heart yearn if his didn't yearn
Isn't that what love is
Isn't that how the heart speaks

This is what she thought
This is what she yearned
This is what she told herself

Her heart could not lie
Her experience could not lie
Her trembling lips could not lie
Her heart was connected to his
This is what she thought

So she stayed in hope
So she stayed entranced
So she stayed in dreams
She stayed in dreams with the man from India

SECTION VI – BOWLING FOR COLUMBINE

BEAD XXIV

He came again to visit
He came in the summer to visit his child
The man from India came to visit his child

She went to him
She went to pick him up at the airport
She drove two hours to pick him up at the airport

He was not angry with her
He was not angry with her regarding his friend
He understood what she did to his friend, her
former lover

She was happy to see him
Was he happy to see her
She didn't know
She wasn't sure

She drove him back
She drove the man from India back
She brought him back to her home

He would stay in the basement
He would stay in the apartment in the basement
The man from India would stay in the apartment in
the basement

BEAD XXV

He came for his child
He came to be with his child
He wanted something special for his child

He thought of Toronto
He thought of a trip to Toronto with his child
He suggested a trip to Toronto with his child

His child wasn't sure
His child was leary
His child was leary to be with him in Toronto

His child wanted her
His child wanted her to go with them to Toronto
His child would go if she went with them to
Toronto

She wasn't sure
She wasn't sure if she should go
She wasn't sure if she should go with them to
Toronto

She went with them
She went with his child
She went with him
She went with him and his child to Toronto

She drove
She drove them with her car
She drove them with her car to Toronto

They arrived
In Toronto they arrived
In Toronto they arrived at the Royal York

His child was happy
His child was in awe
His child was in awe of the Royal York

They shared a room
They shared a room at the Royal York
They shared a room at the Royal York in Toronto

She slept with her
She slept with his child
She slept with his child in Toronto

He was happy with that
The man from India was happy
The man from India was happy to be with her and his child

They walked
All over the city they walked
All over the city they saw stores
All over the city they bought clothes

They swam
In the pool they swam
In the pool of the Royal York they swam

They showered
She and his child showered
She and his child showered by the pool
She and his child showered by the pool of the Royal York

She washed her hair
She washed her long black hair
She washed his child's long black hair

They created bubbles
Lather upon lather they created bubbles
Lather upon lather they created bubbles with her hair

They laughed
Through the bubbles they laughed
Through the lather they laughed
Through the bubbles and lather they laughed
Through the lather and bubbles she and his child laughed

BEAD XXVI

They left Toronto
They left for Niagara
They left to visit Niagara on the Lake
She and his child and the man from India went to
visit Niagara on the Lake

They saw plays there
They saw plays at Niagara on the Lake
They saw two plays at Niagara on the Lake

She chose the plays
She chose the plays that they would see
She chose the plays that they would see at Niagara
on the Lake

They saw the plays
They saw the plays that she chose
They saw the plays that she chose at Niagara on the
Lake
They saw Blood Relations and Misalliance at
Niagara on the Lake

They stayed at a bed and breakfast
She and the man from India and his child stayed at a
bed and breakfast
They stayed at a bed and breakfast at Niagara on the
Lake

It overlooked the river
The bed and breakfast overlooked a river
The bed and breakfast overlooked a river at Niagara
on the Lake

They watched the river
When his child was asleep they watched the river
She and the man from India watched the river when
his child slept

She loved him
Or she thought she loved him
She thought she loved the man from India

He knew
He knew she loved him
The man from India knew she loved him

It was evening
It was evening when his child slept
It was evening when his child slept in her bed at the
bed and breakfast

She wanted him
She wanted to be alone with him
She wanted to be alone with him without his child

This was her chance
This was her chance to be alone with him
She saw her chance to be alone with the man from India

They went for a walk
They went for a walk along the river
She and the man from India went for a walk along the river

He was happy
The man from India was happy
He told her he was happy

He felt like a kid
The man from India felt like a kid
He told her she made him feel like a happy kid

He felt free
The man from India felt free
He told her she set him free

They talked
They talked about love
They talked about sex

She wanted to make love to him

Did he want that
Did he want to make love to her
Did he tease her or did he really want her

He talked
He talked about India
He talked about India to her
He invited her to India
He invited her to come to India for Christmas

She didn't respond
She didn't know
She didn't know what she meant to him
She didn't know why he wanted her in India for
Christmas

She loved him
He knew she loved him
He knew she loved him in every way
He knew she wanted him
The man from India knew she wanted him

He teased her
He teased to tame her
He teased to silence her
He teased to distract her

She didn't know
She didn't know this dance
She didn't know this dance of love
She didn't know the steps to this dance of love
All she knew was she wanted him

BEAD XXVII

She became anxious
She became anxious with the man from India
She became anxious since she didn't know what he wanted
She became anxious since she didn't know if he wanted her

She waited
She had to wait
She had to wait for him
She had to wait for the man from India

Morning came
It was time to leave
It was time to leave the river
It was time to leave the plays
It was time to leave their bed and breakfast

She drove
She drove them back
She drove them back to the child's mother
She drove them back to his apartment
She drove them back to his apartment in her home

BEAD XXVIII

He was in her home
He was in her apartment
He was in her apartment in her home
He was alone in her apartment in her home

She was happy he was there
She was happy to talk with him
She was happy to walk with him
She was happy to share her life with him

His child was away
His child did not distract him
His child left him alone to be with her

They walked
They walked to a movie
They walked to a movie house nearby

They saw a movie
They saw a recent movie
They saw *Bowling for Columbine*

It was not a pleasant movie
It was not a gentle movie
It was not a romantic movie

They left the movie
They walked in silence after the movie
They were left in their own thoughts after the movie

He was uncomfortable
He was uncomfortable with the movie
He walked in front of her after the movie
The man from India walked in front of her from the movie house

She was lost
She was lost in thought
She was thinking of him
She wanted to make love to him

She watched him
She watched him in front of her
She watched him walking in front of her
She watched him pull away from her
She watched as the man from India pulled away from her

They arrived
They arrived at her house
Silently they arrived at her house

She wanted to reach him
She wanted him to want her
She wanted him to play her
She wanted him to play with her

She played music
In her home she played music
In her home she played Liona Boyd
In her home they listened to the guitar of Liona Boyd

She danced
She danced to her music
She danced to the music of Liona Boyd

He sat
He sat in silence
He sat in silence and watched
He sat in silence and watched her dance to Liona Boyd

She danced
She danced and moved to him
She danced to get near to him
She danced and sat on him

He looked at her
From a distant world he looked at her

From a distant world his lingam rose
From a distant world his lingam got hard

He spoke to her
From a distant world he spoke to her
From a distant world he asked her
Do you want sex or do you want to make love
From a distant world he asked her sex or love

She looked at him
She looked at the man from India
On his lap she looked at him
On his lap she told him I want to make love

That won't happen he said
From a distant world he told her
From a distant he told her it would just be sex

He pushed her
He pushed her off him
He pushed her away from him
He left
The man from India left
The man from India went to his apartment
He went to his apartment in her house
She sat
In a daze she sat
In a daze she turned off the music
In a daze she went to her room

She wondered
In the quiet she wondered
In the quiet of her room she wondered
In the quiet of her room she wondered about their talk
In the quiet of her room she wondered about their talk by the river

She felt cheated
In her room she felt cheated
In her room she felt angry
In her room she felt betrayed

She got up
She got up and left her room
She got up and went to him
She went to him in the apartment
She went to him in the apartment in her house

She knocked on his door
Determined-she knocked on his door
Betrayed she knocked on his door
Hurt she knocked on his door

He answered
From his bed he answered
From his bed he asked her in

She told him
She told him I want sex
She told him I want you in me
She told him I want to feel you in me

She climbed
Into the bed she climbed
Onto him she climbed

She danced
Onto him she danced
Onto him she danced on the bed

She felt
She felt his lingam rise
She felt his lingam rise beneath her
She felt his lingam grow hard beneath her

Do you want
She asked him
Do you want to enter she asked him
Do you want to enter me she asked him

In the dark he responded
In the dark he said no
In the dark with his hard lingam he said no

In the dark she went off him
In the dark she lay beside him
In the dark they were silent

She was breathing
She was breathing hard
Beside him she was breathing hard

She wanted him
She wanted him beside her
Though she wanted to come she was happy to be
with him

He knew
He knew she wanted to come
He knew she wanted him inside her

He touched her
With his fingers he touched her
With his fingers he went inside her
With his fingers he played with her

She breathed
She breathed harder
She breathed out loud
She breathed until she came

He was glad
He satisfied her
He was glad he satisfied her

He turned his back
He turned his back from her
He turned his back away from her

She stayed
She stayed with him
She stayed to be with him
She stayed to be next to him

She kissed
She kissed his back
In the dark she kissed his back
In the dark she was happy to be with him

BEAD XXIX

Morning came and with it light
Morning drove away the darkness
Morning found them together
Morning found her next to him

They got up
They got up from the bed
In silence they got up from the bed

She walked
She walked in front of him
In silence she walked in front of him
In silence she was humbled
In silence she left the room
In silence they left the basement

She turned to him
She turned to thank him
She turned to thank him out of shame and rejection
Out of shame and rejection she thanked him
Out of shame and rejection she didn't show her
truth

She thanked him
She thanked him for letting her stay with him
She thanked him for letting her lie with him
She thanked him to make him feel good
She thanked him while she was dying

He was silent
He was silent to her words
He was silent to her gratitude
He was silent to her person

He was blind
He was blind to her truth
He was blind to her humiliation
He was blind to her rejection

He praised himself
He praised himself for his control
He praised himself for his discipline
He praised himself for his focus

Hard as he was he stayed in control
Hard as he was he stayed disciplined
Hard as he was he stayed focused

His words stung
His words pierced
His words broke her heart
His words broke an already shattered heart

She was confused
She was angry
She was rejected
She was embarrassed
She was ashamed
She was feeling too many things
She was unwinding too many hurts

She wanted to cry
She wanted to run away
She wanted to run away from him
She wanted run away to hide her tears

And so she ran
She ran from her house
She ran to her car
She ran to her car and drove

She drove to a friend's house
She drove to her friend's house to cry
She drove to her friend's house to share her tears

She told her friend about her night
She told her friend about her shame
She told her friend about her desire
She told her friend about his words

Her friend saw her tears
Her friend felt her shame

Her friend knew her pain
Her friend listened in vain

Let him go her friend told her
Ask him to leave her friend advised her
He plays with your feelings her friend explained to her
He shouldn't stay her friend reprimanded her

Her friend gave her tea
Her friend calmed her down
Her friend calmed her tears

She stopped crying
She started listening
She started hearing
She started taking her friend's advice

She would ask him to leave
She would ask him to leave right away
She would ask him to not come back

She thought about him
She thought about their time
She thought about the unveiling

Was this love
Was this pain part of love
Was this pain part of being open

Was this pain part of being vulnerable

How could she love him
How could she love him if he didn't love her
How could she be with him if he didn't want to be
with her
How could she share with him if he didn't share
with her

The drive back was cruel
The drive back to her house was cruel
The drive back to see him was cruel

She arrived
She arrived at her house
She arrived at the home he was sharing

She saw him
She saw her in her home
She saw him having tea in her home

She was silent
She had much to say in silence
She opened her mouth in silence

She spoke
She spoke the words
She spoke the words she didn't want to say

She asked him to leave
She asked him to leave her house
She asked him to leave her home

He was devastated
He was humiliated
He had never been treated this way

He asked for time
He asked for time to arrange his things
He asked for time to arrange his schedule

She allowed this time
She allowed the time for his things
She allowed the time for his schedule

The next few days were difficult
The next few days were tense
The next few days were spoken in distant tones

She never told him
She never told him her truth
She never told him her humiliation
She never told him her rejection

He never told her
He never told her his reason
He never told her why they didn't play

He left
He left for a hotel
He left to stay at a nearby hotel

She was devastated
She was devastated with his leaving
She was devastated to lose him
She was devastated to lose his friendship

How can you lose something you never had
How can you lose a love you never had
How can you lose a friend you never had

Why did she feel so terrible
Why did she feel so small
Why did she feel so broken
She still wanted him
She still felt connected to him
She still wanted to be close to him

She was the one who made the mistake
She was the one who was pushing
She was the one wanting someone she couldn't have

She called him
She called him at his hotel
She called to see him

She took him out
She took him out to dinner
She took him and his child out to dinner
She took him and his child out to dinner to
apologize

He was shaken
She was shaken
Whatever they had was shaken
Whatever connective ribbon they had was torn
The connective ribbon was torn and nothing could
mend it

He left for India
He left for his people
He left for his heat

She did not see him off
She would never see him
She would never speak to him

She broke down
She broke down and cried
She broke down and cried and cried

She felt severed
She felt her arm had been severed
She felt her arm had been severed and nothing
could replace it

SECTION VII – GOING TO INDIA

BEAD XXX

She couldn't stop thinking of him
She couldn't stop seeing him
She couldn't stop dreaming of him

It had been three years
It had been three years since he left
It had been three years since he refused her
It had been three years since he refused to play with her

She wondered
She wondered about his refusal
She wondered about his pride
She wondered about his fear

Was he afraid to love her
Was he afraid to be with her
Was he afraid to lose himself inside her

She wanted to understand
She wanted to know
She wanted to let him go

She emailed him
She phoned him
She connected with him again

He responded
He wanted to connect again
He wanted to see her again

She decided
She decided to see him
She decided to see him in India

She made arrangements
She made arrangements to go
She made arrangements to go to India
She made arrangements to see him in India

She wanted to forget
She wanted to forget that fatal night
She wanted to forget her severed arm
She wanted to forgive
She wanted to forgive him
She wanted to forgive him for rejecting her

She wanted to be friends
She wanted to be friends with him
She wanted to be close to him
She wanted to be close to him as friends

She was lying
She was lying to herself
She was lying to herself about him

She wanted him
She wanted him to love her
She wanted him to make love to her

She arrived
She arrived at the airport in India
She arrived alone at the airport in India

He did not go to the airport
He did not go to greet her
He did not go to see her

He sent his driver
He sent his driver to pick her up
He sent his driver to pick her up from the airport

He was hosting her
He was hosting her as she hosted him
He was hosting her in India as she hosted him in Canada

His driver took her
His driver took her to his house
His driver took her to the house where she would stay

She saw him
She saw him in his office
She saw him in his office in his house

He was being polite
He was being careful
He was being careful not to reveal himself

He showed her
He showed her room
He showed her room in his house

He did not embrace
He did not smile
He did not forgive
He did not forget
He did not show warmth or affection

She made a mistake
She made a mistake in coming
She made a mistake in coming to India

Why did she come
Why did she come to see him
Why did she come to see him again

Will he humiliate her
Will he humiliate her as he was humiliated
Will he throw her out like he was thrown out

She sensed his attitude
She sensed his way of being
She sensed his anger

She had to go
She had to stay at a hotel
She had to stay where she felt safe

She told him she was leaving
She told him she wouldn't stay
She told him she wouldn't stay with him that way

He was quiet
He didn't respond
He took her bags into her room
In silence he took her bags into her room

You can stay
You can stay he finally said
You can stay here as I have stayed with you

She went into her room
She unpacked inside her room
She got ready for bed inside her room

Morning came quickly
Morning came with the heat

Morning came with the sounds of the temples

He waited for her
He waited to have breakfast
He waited to have breakfast with her in the kitchen

His cook served breakfast
His cook served breakfast to her
His cook served breakfast to her in a friendly manner

The conversation was formal
The conversation was polite
The conversation was one between strangers

There was no catching up
There was no sharing of the past
There was no openness of friendship

He left after his meal
He left for his office
He left to go and work in his office

She would see him again
She would see him again at lunch
She would see him come from his office and have lunch

She was hoping
She was hoping he would be different
She was hoping he would be open with her at lunch

She was alone
She was in her room alone
She was organizing her clothes alone

She was preparing her work
She was preparing her workshops
She was preparing to give workshops in India

It was time for lunch
It was time for him to come
It was time for him to share a meal with her

He was the same
He was formal
He was polite
He had the same unspoken conversation

She hated him for this
She hated herself for being there
She hated herself for being in this situation

They were not friends
They were not friends who supported each other
They were not friends who knew each other
They were not friends who cared

They were strangers
They were strangers playing at friendship
They were strangers playing at conversation
They were strangers playing with formality

Gone were the walks
Gone were the talks
Gone were the travels
Gone were the secrets they shared

He went back to his work
She went back to her room
He went back to make money
She went back to spend money
He went to supervise people
She was preparing to teach people

She knew it was going to be difficult
She knew it was going to take time
She knew it was going to take patience to win his trust

She had to wait
She had to wait for him to open up
She had to wait for him to forgive her
She had to wait for him to accept her

Supper time came and he was the same
The formality was the same
The politeness was the same

She made a choice
She chose to accept
She chose to accept the politeness
She chose to accept the formality

She traveled far
She traveled thousands of miles to be with him
She traveled to be with him
She traveled to wait
So she would wait

BEAD XXXI

She needed a phone
She needed a phone to work
She needed a phone to reach
She needed a phone to be reached

He promised to help her
He promised to give her a phone
He promised to give her a phone so she could work

They went off
They went off to get a phone
They went off to get her an Indian phone
They went off to a Reliance store

It took time to get the phone
It took time to set up the phone
It took time to register the phone

She didn't mind
He didn't mind
They used the time to walk
They used the time to walk the streets
They used the time to walk the circle

The used the time to watch the traffic
They used the time to be together

His guard had come down
His guard had come down a little
His guard had come down enough to be playful

He teased her
He teased her like he used to
He teased her like he used to before that fateful night

They laughed
For the first time in a long time
They laughed

She felt good
She felt good to see him laugh
She felt good to see him enjoying himself
She felt good to see him enjoying her presence
She felt good to think there was some hope

BEAD XXXII

He brought her to his haveli
He brought her to his haveli in a village
He wanted to show her the haveli in the village

He treated her
He treated her nicely
He treated her with gentleness

She was happy
She was happy to be with him
She was happy to be shown the haveli
She was happy he was showing her the haveli in the village

He had a meeting
He had a meeting to attend
He had an important meeting to attend
He chose not to attend the important meeting

She felt awkward
She felt she was taking his time
She felt she was taking too much of his time

She insisted he go
She insisted he go the meeting
She insisted the meeting was more important then her

He was upset
He was upset with her
He was upset as he wanted the evening for her
He was upset as he planned the evening for her

She wanted to please him
He wanted to please her
Neither pleased each other

Why did he mention the meeting
Why did he mention the meeting to her
Why did he not remain silent about the meeting

It was her fault
It was her fault for not being thankful
It was her fault for not seeing he made her a priority

She didn't think herself worthy
She didn't think herself worthy of being a priority
She didn't think herself worthy of being a priority for him

He brought her home
He brought her to his house with his office

He brought her to his house as he went to the
meeting

She waited for him
She waited for him to return
She waited for him to return from his meeting

The next evening would be their last for a while
He was leaving for business
She was leaving to do workshops

He took her out
He took her out to the city
He drove her around in his city

The streets were full
The streets were full of people
The streets were full of people and weddings

It was time for weddings
It was time for couples
It was time for families
It was time for lots and lots of weddings

They saw parades
They saw parades for weddings
They saw parades with people carrying lanterns
They saw parades with people playing music
They saw parades with the groom on horseback

To her everything was magical
To her everything was enchanting
To her even the hotel lights were mystical

She was happy
She was happy to see him be himself again
She was happy to see him as the person he used to be

In the morning he was packing
In the morning he was packing to leave
He was packing to attend to his business

She watched him pack
She watched him pack and meditate
She watched him pack and meditate to go on his trip

He kissed her
He kissed her in front of the statue of Shiva
He kissed her on the cheek in front of the statue of Shiva

She watched him drive off
She watched him drive off in his car
She watched him drive off to his destination

She touched her cheek
She touched the cheek he kissed
She touched the cheek and she remembered
She touched her cheek and she remembered the
moment

He went off to Mumbai
She went off to Hyderabad
She would return in five weeks
She would return and see him
She would return and he would see her

BEAD XXXIII

She was back
She was back after five weeks
She was back in his house after five weeks

His child was in his house
His child was visiting him in his house
She was happy to see his child in his house

He had another visitor
He had another visitor in his house
He had another visitor with his child in his house

His visitor was a woman
His visitor was a buyer
His visitor was a pretty buyer he had known for years

He was free with his visitor
He was easy with his buyer
He was happy with his blonde-haired buyer

She didn't know what to think
She didn't know how to feel

She didn't know who this buyer was to him

She was jealous
She was jealous of this buyer
She was jealous of him and his buyer
She was jealous of him and his blonde-haired buyer

He brought them to his farm
He brought them to his farm in the village
He brought them to see his cows and trees in his farm

Everyone was polite
Everyone had a good time
Everyone saw how proud he was of his farm

His child left
His child went back to school
His child went back to Delhi

His buyer was leaving
His buyer was finished with her business
His buyer was returning to her home
He arranged a meal
He arranged a meal for his buyer
He was very happy to arrange a meal for his buyer

He liked his buyer
He was carefree with his buyer

He was carefree and laughed with his buyer

She was alone with him
She was alone with him after his buyer left
She was on edge with him after his buyer left

He was on edge with her
He was on edge and forgot her name
He was on edge and called her by his buyer's name

She was leaving
She was leaving the next day
She was leaving the next day but couldn't sleep

She had to speak with him
She had to let him know
She had to let him know how foolish she'd been

She woke him up
Early in the morning she woke him up
She told him she felt foolish
She told him she made a mistake in coming
She told him she felt he didn't like her

In silence he listened
In silence she left him
In silence she went to pack her bags
In silence she packed to leave

Her bags were packed
She was ready to leave
She was ready to leave his house
She was ready to leave him

He caught up with her
He caught up to respond to her
He caught up to share his thoughts

He agreed
He agreed he didn't like her
He agreed he didn't like her bossy ways
He agreed he didn't like her calling attention to herself

She was hurt
She was devastated
She was holding back her tears

She didn't know
She didn't know her behavior bothered him
She didn't know her suggestions irritated him

He was careful with her
He weighed his words carefully with her
He carefully asked what she wanted from him

She wanted to be with him
She wanted to share with him

She wanted to be friends with him

Through her tears she told him
Through her tears she felt him
Through her tears she conveyed her wants

She told him she would change
She told him she would change for him
She told him she would go to hell for him

She wanted him to be nice to her
She wanted him to be open to her
She wanted him to be carefree with her

Those times were few he said
Those times were gone he said
Those times were when he trusted he said
Those times were when he trusted he said

He didn't like her emails
He didn't like the emails she sent
He didn't like the emails she sent those past three years
He didn't like the emails expressing her feelings

She was a fool
She was an idiot
She was crying
She was crying for a man who didn't care

BEAD XXXIV

It was time for her to leave
It was time to take him out
It was time to say their last goodbyes
It was time to politely thank him
It was time to politely thank him for his hospitality

He didn't want to go out
He didn't want to go out with her
He made excuses to not go out with her

She listened
She knew

He didn't want to please her
He didn't want to forget
He didn't want to forgive
He didn't want her to be his friend

They stayed home
They spent their last meal at home
They had their last meal cooked in his house

He planned their meal
He planned their last meal

He planned their last meal in his house

His cook prepared their meal
His cook prepared a simple last meal
His cook prepared a simple last meal in his house

Their last meal was chicken
Their last meal was chicken with rice
Their last meal was a tasty chicken with rice

She was glad
She was glad they didn't go out
She was glad they didn't go out to be distracted

It gave her time
It gave her courage
It gave her the reality check she needed

In his house she could wash away the tears
In his house she could gather her strength
In his house she could gather the strength to let him go

She took this journey for him
She took this journey for her
She took this journey to find love
She took this journey to understand love
She took this journey to find love in herself